SERMON OUTLINES
for

Funerals and Other Special Services

D0062568

The Bryant Sermon Outline Series

A HAPPY LIFE

Psalm 32

1. An experience of PARDON (vv. 1–5).
2. An enjoyment of PROTECTION (vv. 6–7).
3. An entering into God's PURPOSE (v. 8).

Author Unknown

SOME IMPOSSIBLE THINGS

Mark 9:23

1. None shall see God without holiness (Eph. 5:5; Heb. 12:14).
2. None can please Him without faith (Heb. 11:6).
3. None can find a lie in God (Jer. 10:10; Titus 1:2).
4. None can enter the kingdom of God without the new birth (John 3:5).
5. None can escape if they reject the Gospel (Heb. 2:3).
6. None can be saved after death (Heb. 9:27).
7. None can be condemned if they believe in Christ Jesus (John 5:24; Acts 16:31; Rom. 10:9).

A. B. Carrero

In the Heart

A missionary in Africa, translating the gospel of John into Songhai, could not find a word to express "believe." He took his problem to a native Christian. The man thought a few minutes and then suggested, "Doesn't it mean to hear in my heart?"

Reader's Digest

WHAT IS YOUR LIFE?

James 4:13–17

Introduction

This is the great question of every man who thinks seriously. It is the point of departure for either happiness or misery. For a satisfactory answer to this challenging question we do well to consult the Word of God.

I. Life Is a Gift of God
A. "In him we live, and move, and have our being" (Acts 17:28).

B. "Ye are not your own" (1 Cor. 6:19–20).

II. Life Is a Trust
This fact is clearly set forth in Matthew 25:14–29.

III. Life Is a Journey Not Measured by Miles but by Years

IV. Life Is an Investment
A. Matthew 10:39; John 12:25.

B. It is not small investment for small gain; but total investment and total gain, or total loss.

Fred Reedy

A Striking Difference
A missionary in India had been speaking about the "Water of Life," and pointed to a fountain close by where people were drinking and filling their pots. A Moslem bystander said, "Your religion may be compared to a little stream of water, but Islam is like a great sea."

"Yes," replied the missionary, "but there is just this difference: men drink sea water and die of thirst, while they drink of the living water and live."

Author Unknown

DAVID AND THE GIANT

1 Samuel 17:45–51

Introduction

David's older brother envied him. Eliab's attitude was that of contempt. He thought David would be more in place under a tree playing his harp.

Lions and bears fight differently; neither was a match for David.

David picked up five smooth stones for his sling. They mean:

I. Stone One—A Clear-cut Break with Sin
A. David was clean and clear.
B. He reflected the first psalm ("In his law doth he . . .").
C. In his life was no ill spirit toward his parents.
D. He won the title—"A man after God's own heart."

II. Stone Two—A Clear-cut Relationship with God
A. There was no halfway experience for him.
B. We know him because he was all out for God.
C. The Lord wants to make Himself real to us all.
    1. Real repentance.
    2. Real forsaking of sin.
    3. Real praying through.
    4. Real witness of the Spirit.

III. Stone Three—Right of Way for the Holy Spirit
God alone makes people strong in the right way.
A. The Holy Spirit and wholeness.
B. The Holy Spirit and a clean heart.
C. The Holy Spirit and harmonious living.

IV. Stone Four—Dependence upon God
David said much about the Lord being his strength.
A. He relied on God to make him strong.
B. He relied on God to keep him true.
C. He relied on God in overcoming his enemies.

V. Stone Five—Full Consecration to God
A. Christ wants full control of your life.
B. Christ wants to help plan your life.
C. Christ has worthy objectives for your life.
D. Christ will make your life the greatest blessing to yourself and others.

Nelson Mink

THE ORDAINED MEMORIAL

Luke 22:19–20

I. The Main Object of the Supper Is a Personal Memorial

"In remembrance of *me*." We are to remember not so much His doctrines, or precepts, as His Person. Remember the Lord Jesus at this Supper—

A. As the trust of your hearts.

B. As the object of your gratitude.

C. As the Lord of your conduct.

D. As the joy of your lives.

II. The Memorial Itself Is Striking

A. *Simple*, and therefore like Himself, who is transparent and unpretentious truth. Only bread broken and wine poured out.

B. *Frequent*—"as oft as ye drink it," and so pointing to our constant need. He intended the Supper to be often enjoyed.

C. *Universal*, and so showing the need of all. "Drink ye all of it." In every land, all His people are to eat and drink at this table.

D. His death is the best memory of Himself, and it is by showing forth *His death* that we remember *Him*.

III. The Object Aimed At Is Itself Inviting

A. We may come to it, though we forget Him often.

B. We may come, though others may be forgetful of Him. We come not to judge *them*.

C. H. Spurgeon

THE GIFT DIVINE

John 6:48

This message of Jesus is prefaced by the desire of the people to ◌ᵉ and be with Jesus (vv. 22–27).

1. Jesus, the Bread of Life

He startled His listeners by His declaration, "I am that bread of life," etc. (vv. 47–59).

The effect of the saying—"This is a hard saying" (v. 60)—caused many of His disciples to forsake Him (v. 66).

The Twelve, however, were inspired to give one of their great confessions of Him: "To whom shall we go? Thou hast the words of eternal life. And we believe and are sure that thou art that Christ, the Son of the living God" (vv. 68–69).

II. Jesus and the Passover

(Luke 22:15–20)

Perhaps a year after Jesus' discourse on the Bread of Life, He expressed an ardent desire to eat the Passover with His disciples (v. 15). Evidently this desire was to give to them a new meaning of the old rite and to substitute the Lord's Supper as a symbol of the fulfillment of this old Passover. Here He would reveal what He meant by His being "the bread of life."

III. Jesus the Divine Gift, Emphasized by the Lord's Supper

His broken body is our spiritual bread indeed; His shed blood is our spiritual life. Thus the greatest of all sacraments was instituted as a perpetual reminder of His death and as a constant revelation of our life in Him. The emblems used are broken bread and the fruit of the vine, the wine. This sacrament has been observed and held most sacred by the church throughout the Christian era.

IV. The Theology of the Sacrament

We believe, since Christ was still alive and no blood had as yet been spilled when He took the bread and broke it and passed it, also the cup and passed it, saying, "This is my body which is given for you," and, "This cup is the new testament in my blood, which is shed for you," that these elements become a sacred symbol of deep spiritual facts—as if Jesus said, "As this bread is to your physical body, so My body is to the spiritual health of those who believe and partake of Me." The cup is the symbol of His blood shed for our redemption and that through that blood we now know His pardon; also that His broken body is a symbol of our constant participation in Him for spiritual life.

Thus we have the Gift Divine—Jesus Christ Himself. Thus by our partaking of these emblems we symbolize what He meant when He said: "Whoso eateth my flesh, and drinketh my blood, has eternal life; and I will raise him up at the last day" (John 6:54), and, ". . . dwelleth in me, and I in him" (v. 56).

And so when we kneel before God in this sacrament of Holy Communion, we may be assured that our every act of adoration and love is seen and accepted by our blessed, crucified, but risen Lord, who is at the right hand of God interceding in our behalf.

J. Paul Downey

THE OBJECTS OF THE LORD'S SUPPER

1. **Commemoration**
   "In remembrance" (Luke 22:19).

2. **Representation**
   "The bread which we break" (1 Cor. 10:16).

3. **Proclamation**
   Speaks of His death (Luke 22:20).

4. **Communication**
   "All partake of that one bread" (1 Cor. 10:17).

5. **Anticipation**
   "Till he come" (1 Cor. 11:26).

Charles Inglis

Simplicity
The Philippian jailor was not counseled to look up the scientific reason for earthquakes, nor advised to move into some other tenement. "Believe on the Lord Jesus Christ, and thou shalt be saved."

Author Unknown

THE SIGNIFICANCE OF THE LORD'S SUPPER

1 Corinthians 11:23–29

Introduction
The Lord's Supper is misunderstood by some. It is an ordinance, a sacrament—solidly scriptural, rich in significance and experience.

I. His Institution (v. 23)
Begun, not by apostles nor by church Fathers, but by Jesus Himself.

II. His Incarnation (v. 24)
"This is my body . . ."

III. His Crucifixion (v. 24)
"My body broken for you . . . my blood" (1 Peter 1:18–19).

IV. His Invitation (or command) (vv. 24–25)
"This do . . ."

V. His Recollection (vv. 24–25)
"In remembrance of me."

VI. His Proclamation (v. 26)
". . . ye do shew the Lord's death . . ."

VII. His Anticipation (v. 26)
"Till he come."

Conclusion
The Lord's Supper becomes a supper for us by:
Salvation—must first be saved.
Appropriation—by faith, take, eat.
Assimilation—strength for life and service.

B. W. Downing

How Could I Stay Away?
True believers have a longing for the memorials of their Lord. Whitecross tells of one of the converted Greenlanders, who had taken a seal, and rather than be absent from the settlement of the missionaries when the Lord's Supper was to be administered, rode the whole night in his Kayak with the animal in tow. When his exertion was mentioned, he answered, "How could I stay where I was? My soul hungers and thirsts after the Lord and His Communion."

The Illustrator

THE HOLY SUPPER

Luke 22:7–20

Introduction

This holy supper was eaten on the same night that Christ was betrayed and put under arrest.

I. The Holy Passover
A. The disciples had prepared the Passover (v. 8).

B. It was in the upper room of a believer's house in Jerusalem (vv. 11–12).

C. Christ had kept this feast from His youth.

D. This feast commemorated the Exodus from Egypt.

II. Institution of the Holy Communion
A. At the Crucifixion Christ became our Passover sacrifice (1 Cor. 5:7).

B. The communion took the place of the Passover.

C. It is to be observed until Christ comes (1 Cor. 11:26).

D. It is to be done in remembrance of Him (1 Cor. 11:25).

    1. We are to look back to His death.

    2. We are to look forward to His Coming.

III. The Supper
A. He blessed the cup (v. 17).

B. He blessed and broke bread (v. 19).

IV. Who Shall Eat? (1 Cor. 11:27, 33)
A. Christians are to eat.

B. Each man shall be his own judge (vv. 28, 31).

C. He who eats unworthily only condemns himself (v. 29).

D. It is dangerous to partake of this Holy Communion unworthily.

    1. Some were weak and sickly as a penalty (v. 30).

    2. Some died (v. 30).

Conclusion

If we eat and drink unworthily, we are in danger; if we do not eat, we have no life in us (John 6:53).

Master Sermon Outlines

A QUICK LOOK AT THE LORD'S SUPPER

1.	The PERSON we remember	"Me"—the Lord
2.	The FACT we announce	"His death."
3.	The EVENT we wait for	"Until He come."

1,000 Subjects for Speakers and Students

THE LORD'S SUPPER IN PSALM 16:8

The psalmist set the Lord always before him—

1. **As an Object of Trust (v. 1).**

2. **As His Counselor (vv. 7, 11).**

3. **As His Savior (vv: 8, 10–11).**

As we celebrate this supper, we can join the psalmist in worshiping our Savior.

adapted from *Illustrated Sermon Outlines*

Don't Stay Away

A man called his pastor on the telephone and said, "I'm not coming to the Communion service this time. I don't feel prepared; and since I've been sick, I'm so shaky and low in spirits; and somehow I just feel I've failed the Lord so much."

The wise minister answered, "My friend, I'm afraid it's your feelings you are going by. You know there's a good place to prepare, and that's in the secret place of prayer where none but the Lord sees and hears. And no matter what your feelings are, remember 'He ever liveth to make intercession' for you. Don't stay away from the Lord's Table, friend, because of your feelings; that's just what the Devil wants you to do. Meet the Lord at His Table and let it be a time of heart-searching and revival for you. It will be, if you will let it."

Mrs. J. Shields

THE LORD'S SUPPER

Matthew 26:17–30

I. Introduction

It was a tradition of the Jews that in the days of the Messiah they should be redeemed on the very day of their coming out of Egypt. And this was exactly fulfilled, for Christ died the day after the Passover, on which day they began their march.

A. The disciples knew it took some preparation and they asked the question, "Where wilt thou that we prepare the passover?"

B. They ate the Passover according to the law.

C. Jesus gave notice of His knowledge of the treachery that should be among them. Note the feelings of the disciples on this occasion.

1. They were exceedingly sorrowful.
2. They began to inquire, "Lord, is it I?" None of them suspected Judas, but there seems a fear lest it be any one of them.

D. Jesus tells them who the traitor is—he is a familiar friend—"He that dippeth his hand with me in the dish." External communion with Christ in holy ordinances is a great aggravation of our falseness to Him. It is base ingratitude to dip with Christ in the dish and yet betray Him.

II. The Institution of the Lord's Supper

A. The broken bread. The body of Christ is signified and represented by the bread.

1. He blessed the bread—setting it apart for this use by prayer and thanksgiving.
2. He broke the bread—denoting the breaking of His own body. He was bruised for our iniquities.

B. He took the cup—the blood of Jesus is signified and represented by the wine. He took the cup—the cup of grace, the sacramental cup.

1. His command, "Drink ye all of it: for this is my blood of the new testament." Hitherto it has been the blood of animals which was shed for sins; now it is the blood of Jesus.
2. His blood is shed for many for the remission of sins.

3. His promise and hope of a new day—"I will not drink henceforth of this fruit," etc. His earthly career was soon to cease; there would be the coming of the kingdom; this sacrament will then be "new"—fulfilled.
4. They sang a hymn. This is a gospel custom, a practice of worship. They went out to the Mount of Olives, to the Garden for prayer.
   After we have received the Lord's Supper it is always good for us to retire for prayer and meditation—to be alone with God.

J. Paul Downey

PREPARATION FOR COMMUNION

1 Corinthians 11:28

Spiritual inventory is not intended to keep you away, but to help you to go on.

1. **Review your past relationship to the Savior.**

2. **Confess to Christ all known sins and failures, and forsake them.**

3. **Accept the divine forgiveness as provided in the death of Christ for us.**

4. **Rededicate yourself and life to Christ.**

5. **Accept and rely upon Christ as your life.**

adapted from *J. A. Trostle*

THE BODY OF CHRIST

Hebrews 10:5

1. Holy (Isa. 53:9; Luke 1:35; 2 Cor. 5:21).

2. Offered in sacrifice (Heb. 10:10).

3. Given to the smiters (Isa. 50:6; 53:5).

4. Broken on the cross (1 Cor. 11:24).

5. Buried in the grave (John 19:40).

6. Anointed by Mary and Nicodemus (John 12:3; 19:39).

7. Seen after His resurrection (Luke 24:39).

8. Ascended into heaven (Acts 1:9–11; Phil 3:20–21).

9. Discerned in the Communion table (1 Cor. 11:29).

A. B. Carrero

Reminders

Our Lord, who knows our nature perfectly, knows that memory is a light sleeper, starting awake at the slightest knock. A bar of music or some familiar fragrance, and the past is all back with us again. A scrap of writing or a little shoe, and we are wandering through vanished years. Often when we have sinned and fallen and are in peril of the hardened heart, it is in such ways that memory awakes. Hence the simplicity of Christian sacraments. They are not anticipative; they are commemorative. They do not portray One who is unknown; their office is to recall One who has been here. So all that is needed is a bit of bread and a cup of wine on the table—and we remember the Lord's death until He come.

Dr. George H. Morrison

TRUTHS CONNECTED WITH THE HOLY SPIRIT

I. **The Holy Spirit . . .**
   A. Convicts the World (John 16:8–12).
   B. Regenerates the Believing One (John 3:5–7; 1 John 5:7).
   C. Indwells the Child of God (John 14:17).
   D. Seals the Saint (Eph. 1:13).
   E. Is the Comforter and Guide (John 15:26; 16:13).
   F. Is the Unction or Holy Anointing (1 John 2:20).
   G. Is the Earnest of Coming Glory (Eph. 1:14).

II. **The Christian is Exhorted to . . .**
   A. Be Filled with the Spirit (Eph. 5:18).
   B. Pray in the Spirit (Jude 20; Eph. 6:18).
   C. Sing in the Spirit (Eph. 5:19).
   D. Worship in the Spirit (John 4:23; Phil. 3:3).
   E. Walk in the Spirit (Gal. 5:16).
   F. Be Led by the Spirit (Gal. 5:18).
   G. Remember His Body Is the Temple of the Holy Spirit (1 Cor. 6:19).

Twelve Baskets Full

THE HOLY SPIRIT

I. What He Is
A. He Is a Person. "Descended in bodily shape" (Luke 3:22).
B. He Always Existed. "The eternal Spirit" (Heb. 9:14).
C. He Is Omniscient. "Searcheth all things" (1 Cor. 2:10).
D. He Is Omnipresent. "Whither shall I go," etc. (Ps. 139:7–11).
E. He Is Omnipotent. Raised the dead witnesses (Rev. 11:11).

II. His Operations
A. Convinces. "Convince the world of sin" (John 16:8).
B. Quickens. "Quicken . . . by His Spirit" (Rom. 8:11).
C. Indwells. "If the spirit . . . dwell in you" (Rom. 8:9).
D. Comforts. "Another Comforter" (John 14:16–17).
E. Seals. "Sealed with that Holy Spirit" (Eph. 1:13).
F. Reveals. "Revealed . . . by the Spirit" (Eph. 3:5).
G. Sanctifies. "Sanctified . . . by the Spirit" (1 Cor. 6:11).
H. Leads. "Led by the Spirit of God" (Rom. 8:14).
I. Witnesses. "The Spirit itself beareth witness" (Rom. 8:16).

Bible Themes for Busy Workers